The Small Things
by Enda Walsh

Cast

Woman	Valerie Lilley
Man	Bernard Gallagher

Director	Vicky Featherstone
Designer	Neil Warmington
Lighting Designer	Natasha Chivers
Sound Designer	Mat Ort
Voice Coach	Ros Steen

Production Manager	Neil Black
Deputy Stage Manager	Perrine Desproges
Technical Stage Manager	Mat Ort

Press Representative

Emma Schad
07930 308018

Cover Image

Stuart McCaffer
lostdug@hotmail.com

First performed at the Menier Chocolate Factory 28 January 2005.

The playscript that follows was correct at time of going to press, but may have changed during rehearsal.

ENDA WALSH
Writer

Enda Walsh lives in London. He has had seven stage plays produced to date. These include The Ginger Ale Boy, Disco Pigs, Misterman and Bedbound. He has won the Stewart Parker and the George Devine Awards, two Edinburgh Fringe Awards and two Critic's Awards. Disco Pigs and Bedbound have been translated into 18 languages and have had productions throughout Europe. His play Misterman has been in rep at the Schaubuhne in Berlin for three years. He has written two radio plays: Four Big Days in the Life of Dessie Banks for RTE which won the IPA Radio Drama Award and The Monotonous Life of Little Miss P for the BBC which was commended at the Grand Prix Berlin. His latest play The New Electric Ballroom for the Kammerspiele in Munich is currently running as well as a short play for the Zurich Shauspielhaus called Fraternity. He has recently finished a play for the National Theatre's Connections Project called Chatroom. A new play Pondlife Angels opens in Cork in June this year. He wrote the screenplay of the film Disco Pigs which was released in 2002 and is currently under commission for two other films: Miss Emerald Isle and an adaptation of the children's story The Island of the Aunts by Eva Ibbotson. He is also working on a Bobby Sands Project for Film Four to be filmed next year.

NATASHA CHIVERS
Lighting Design

During This Other England Natasha is designing: The Small Things, Mercury Fur, Pyrenees and If Destroyed True. For Paines Plough: The Straits (with Drum Theatre Plymouth & Hampstead Theatre inc. New York tour), On Blindness (with Frantic Assembly & Graeae), The Drowned World, Tiny Dynamite (with Frantic Assembly inc. International Tour). Theatre includes: Urban Legend and The Kindness Of Strangers (Liverpool Everyman 40th anniversary Season), Who's Afraid Of The Big Bad Book? (Soho Theatre), Ma Rainey's Black Bottom and

The Entertainer (Liverpool Playhouse), Very Little Women (Lip Service tour), Hymns (Frantic Assembly/Lyric Hammersmith), The Bomb-itty of Errors (The New Ambassadors/Dublin), The Cherry Orchard and After The Dance (Oxford Stage Company), Playhouse Creatures (West Yorkshire Playhouse), Peepshow (Frantic Assembly, Plymouth Theatre Royal, Lyric Hammersmith), Sell Out (Frantic Assembly), Wit and The Memory Of Water (Stellar Quines), Present Laughter (Bath Theatre Royal Productions).

VICKY FEATHERSTONE
Director

Vicky Featherstone is currently Artistic Director of the National Theatre of Scotland. While Artistic Director of Paines Plough she directed: On Blindness by Glyn Cannon, The Drowned World by Gary Owen (Pearson Best Play, Fringe First), Tiny Dynamite by Abi Morgan (MEN Best Fringe Production), Crazy Gary's Mobile Disco by Gary Owen, Splendour by Abi Morgan (TMA/Barclays Best Director & Best Play, Fringe First & Herald Angel), Riddance by Linda McLean, (Fringe First & Herald Angel), The Cosmonaut's Last Message To The Woman He Once Loved In The Former Soviet Union by David Greig, Crave by Sarah Kane, Sleeping Around by Hilary Fannin, Stephen Greenhorn, Abi Morgan and Mark Ravenhill, and Crazyhorse by Parv Bancil.

BERNARD GALLAGHER
Man

Theatre includes: Christmas (Bush Theatre), Caligula (Donmar), A Christmas Carol, In Celebration, Getting Married, Therese Raquin (Chichester), Richard II/ Coriolanus, School for Wives (Almeida), Enjoy (West Yorkshire), Blue Heart (Out of Joint/Royal Court), The Last Yankee (Bristol Old Vic), The Three Sisters (Out of Joint), The Libertine, Carnival War A-Go-Hot (Royal Court), Hamlet (Bristol), Gaslight (Greenwich), The Black Angel (King's Head), Educating Rita (Young Vic Tour), Fancy Man (Hampstead), El Cid (Half Moon), Loot (Manchester), Roll on 4 O'Clock (Lyric/Palace), The Country Wife (Leatherhead), Breezeblock Park (Whitehall), Weapons of Happiness, Jumpers, National Theatre company 1968-72 (National), Columbus, 'Tis Pity She's A Whore, Julius Caesar, The Alchemist (RSC). TV includes: Heatwave, East Enders, Doctors, Silent Witness, Murder in Mind, Harry, First and Last, Rockliffe's Babies, Casualty, Frankie and Johnnie, Moonfleet, Rolling Home, Bergerac, The Jail Diary of Albie Sachs, The Imitation Game, Eagle of the Ninth (BBC), Midsomer Murders, Rose and Maloney, The Bill (ITV), Bad Girls, Strangers, (Granada), A Wing & a Prayer (Channel 5), Heartbeat, New Statesman, Farrington of the FO (YTV), Wycliffe (HTV), Cows (Pozzitive Films), Thin Blue Line, This is David Lander (Hat Trick), London's Burning (LWT), Brother Cadfael (Central Films), The Chief (Anglia), Count Down to War, Prisoners of Childhood, Relative Strangers (Ch 4), Shine on Harvey Moon (Central).

VALERIE LILLEY
Woman

Valerie trained at the Actors Workshop. Theatre includes: Juno & The Paycock (Gaiety Theatre), Breezeblock Park, Shadow of a Gunman, Pigs Ear (Liverpool Playhouse), Madness in Goa (Oldham Coliseum), The Cherry Orchard, The Card (New Victoria, Stoke), Fen & Faraway, Jane Eyre (Sheffield Crucible), My Mother Said I Never Should, Blood Wedding (Bolton Octagon), Lysistrata (Contact Manchester), Drive On (Lyric Belfast), The Beauty Queen of Leenane (Salisbury Playhouse), Sister Leonid in The True Life Fiction of Mata Hari (Watford Palace Theatre), national tour & two seasons at the Bush (7:84), Flying Blind, Inventing A New Colour (Royal Court), Killing The Cat (Soho Poly at the Royal Court Theatre Upstairs), Factory Girls, Once A Catholic, A Love Song For Ulster, The Mai (Tricycle Theatre), Blue Heart (Royal Court/Out Of Joint), Holy Mothers (Ambassadors), On Raftery's Hill, Loyal Women (Druid Theatre Company/Royal Court). TV includes Scully (Granada), Coronation Street, The Refuge, Final Run, Albion Market, Children of the North, Nice Town, The Riff Raff Element, East Enders, Blood on the Dole (Channel 4), Elidor, Missing Persons, The Famous Five, Sister Mary in The Rag Nymph, First Communion Day, Peak Practice, Hope & Glory (BBC), Anybody's Nightmare (Carlton), Crime & Punishment (BBC), Grange Hill, Serious and Organised, Court Drama, Messiah 3, Courtroom (Mersey TV). Film includes Scrubbers and Priest (Mai Zetterling).

MAT ORT
Sound Designer

Mat trained in Theatre Design and Technology at Bretton Hall College. TSM work for Paines Plough includes The Straits (with Hampstead & Drum Theatre Plymouth), Tiny Dynamite (with Frantic Assembly/Contact Manchester) Other theatre includes: Underworld, Heavenly, (Frantic Assembly - TSM) The Tale That Wags The Dog (Drum Theatre Plymouth and A &BC - CSM), The Chair Women (Scarlet Theatre - Technical Manager).

ROS STEEN
Voice Coach

Trained at RSAMD. As a voice/dialect coach she has worked extensively in Theatre, TV & Film as well as teaching voice at the Royal Scottish Academy of Music and Drama. Recent work includes A Little Bit of Ruff season at the Glasgow Citizens' and the upcoming film Greyfriars Bobby.

NEIL WARMINGTON
Designer

Neil graduated in Fine Art Painting from Maidstone College of Art before attending the Motley theatre design course in London. Neil is designing The Small Things, Pyrenees and If Destroyed True, in our This Other England season. For Paines Plough: The Straits, The Drowned World, Splendour, Riddance, Crazy Horse. Other theatre includes: King Lear (ETT/Old Vic), Ghosts, Don Juan, John Gabriel Borkman, Taming of the Shrew, Love's Labour's Lost (ETT), Woyzeck, The Glass Menagerie, Comedians, Tankred Dorsts Merlin (Royal Lyceum Edinburgh), Full Moon For A Solemn Mass, Family, Passing Places, King of the Fields, Gagarin Way, Slab Boys Trilogy (Traverse/National Theatre), Angels in America (7:84), Life's a Dream, Fiddler on the Roof, Playhouse Creatures, (West Yorkshire Playhouse), Henry V (RSC), Much Ado About Nothing (Queen's London), Sunset Song, Mary Queen of Scots Got Her Head Chopped Off (Theatre Royal, Glasgow), The Life of Stuff (Donmar), Waiting for Godot (Liverpool Everyman),

The Tempest (Contact), Jane Eyre, Desire Under the Elms (Shared Experience), Troilus & Cressida (Opera North), Oedipus Rex (Connecticut State Opera), The Marriage of Figaro (Garsington Opera), Scenes From An Execution, Dumbstruck, Lie Of The Mind (Dundee), Knives in Hens, The Birthday Party (Tag). Neil has also won three TMA Awards for best design, been part of numerous Edinburgh Fringe First productions and has been awarded The Linbury Prize for stage design, and the Sir Alfred Munnings Florence Prize for painting.

PAINES PLOUGH'S THIS OTHER ENGLAND

at the Menier Chocolate Factory
Friday 28 January – Sunday 22 May 2005.

**"If new writing in this country is going to have any far-reaching
significance, then it needs Paines Plough"**
THE INDEPENDENT

This Other England is a ground-breaking body of work marking the 30th anniversary
of new writing powerhouse Paines Plough.

Taking its cue from Melvyn Bragg's BBC Radio 4 series The Routes of English, Paines
Plough commissioned eight outstanding voices of theatre to think about English as
a language and how it shapes our identity. This season we premiere the first four of
these commissions which offer a theatrical cross-section of where we are now. This
is the start of an extraordinary series, we hope you will join us and be a part of it from
the beginning.

**"Paines Plough remains at the Pinnacle of
New British theatre."** METRO

An exceptional season deserves a great venue and we are proud to be presenting
these productions at London's most inspiring new venue; the Menier Chocolate
Factory, which offers a unique space minutes from London Bridge with an atmospheric
bar and delicious candlelit restaurant.

"The legendary Paines Plough"
THE INDEPENDENT

This season would not have been possible without the vision and commitment of our
co-producing partners. For Mercury Fur; Drum Theatre Plymouth. For Pyrenees; Tron
Theatre Glasgow and in association with Watford Palace Theatre. For If Destroyed
True; Dundee Rep Theatre. Each production is appearing at its associated venue as
well as in London during the season.

THE SMALL THINGS by Enda Walsh
Menier Chocolate Factory, London. Fri 28 Jan - Sun 27 Feb.
MERCURY FUR by Philip Ridley
Drum Theatre Plymouth. Thurs 10 Feb - Sat 26 Feb.
Menier Chocolate Factory, London. Tues 1 Mar - Sun 27 Mar.
PYRENEES by David Greig
Tron Theatre, Glasgow. Wed 9 Mar - Sat 26 Mar.
Menier Chocolate Factory, London. Tues 29 Mar - Sun 24 Apr.
Watford Palace Theatre. Tues 26 Apr - Sat 30 Apr.
IF DESTROYED TRUE by Douglas Maxwell
Dundee Rep Theatre. Sat 9 Apr - Sat 23 Apr.
Menier Chocolate Factory, London. Tues 26 Apr - Sun 22 May.

Supported by the Peggy Ramsay Foundation

PAINES PLOUGH PRESENTS... ENGAGE

Engage: Take part, participate, involve (a person or his or her attention), intensely, employ (a person), begin a battle with, bring (a mechanism) into operation.

engage: Wild Lunch Funsize
Paines Plough and Half MoonYoung People's Theatre are developing short plays for little people by grown-up writers - Jennifer Farmer, Dennis Kelly, Abi Morgan, Chloe Moss, Gary Owen and Mark Ravenhill. Performances will be at lunchtime on Tues 22 Mar, Wed 23 Mar, Thurs 24 Mar, Thurs 31 Mar, Fri 1 April and Sat 2 April. Find a child under 7 and bring them along. Tickets are available from Half Moon on 020 7709 8900 and tickets@halfmoon.org.uk

engage: Battle
Chaired by Michael Billington. Leading playwrights duel with each other to persuade the audience that their chosen dramatist is the greatest of all time. You decide who wins. Battle commences at 6.30pm on Fri 4 Mar and Fri 29 April. [FREE]

engage: Later
Curated by Mark Ravenhill. A series of surprising, late night theatrical events dotted throughout the season. Mark will be taking his pick of performers and artists and presenting a taste of their latest work. Performances will be post-show on Fri 25 Feb, Fri 25 Mar, Fri 22 Apr and Fri 20 May. [FREE]

engage: Explore
A chance to take a look behind-the-scenes of This Other England – come down to the Chocolate Factory. We will be receiving visitors from 11am – 3pm on Wed 9 Feb and Wed 6 April [FREE]

engage: Discuss
Each post show discussion will feature a contribution from a guest expert. [FREE]

The Small Things	I speak therefore I am	Thurs 17 Feb
Mercury Fur	When Words Lose Meaning	Thurs 17 Mar
Pyrenees	Language and Identity	Thurs 14 Apr
If Destroyed True	Language and Technology	Thurs 12 May

engage: Whispers of Britain
Assistant Director Hamish Pirie in a dynamic theatrical lecture recounts his pilgrimage to take a Chinese whisper around the British Isles. Performances will be at lunchtimes on Thurs 12 and Fri 13 May. [FREE]

engage: Masterclasses
A new series of our successful writers' masterclasses will take place during the second half of This Other England. Full details of dates, titles and workshop leaders will be available at the start of the season.

engage: Schools
We will be offering a limited number of workshops for schools to accompany each of the productions. If you would like to find out more about our provision for schools please contact Susannah on 020 7240 4533.

Free events are not ticketed and seating is limited so please arrive at the venue in plenty of time to ensure your place.

More information on the participants and content of these events will be available nearer to the time. If you would like to be the first to find out more please email Susannah@painesplough.com with 'e-ngage' in the subject line.

PAINES PLOUGH

"The legendary Paines Plough" Independent

Paines Plough is an award-winning nationally and internationally renowned touring theatre company, specialising exclusively in the commissioning and development of contemporary playwrights and the production of their work on stage. We tour the work throughout Britain and overseas ensuring the widest possible audience can benefit from it.

We work with both new and experienced writers and develop plays with a ground-breaking and highly respected programme of workshops and readings. In order to inspire new playwrights and find new audiences, we also have a pioneering education and outreach programme which focuses on encouraging people to write.

Our writers are encouraged to be courageous in their work, to challenge our notions of theatre and the society we live in.

Paines Plough was founded in 1974 by director John Adams and playwright David Pownall to commission and tour new plays. At the time it was the only such company in England and quickly became known as The Writers Company, for its commitment to placing the writer at the centre of the company.

Although Paines Plough has changed direction with the vision of each Artistic Director, there has always been a consistency in commissioning the best writers of each generation and touring this work nationally. These include David Pownall, Stephen Jeffreys, Heathcote Williams, Terry Johnson, Tony Marchant, Pam Gems, Mark Ravenhill, Sarah Kane, Abi Morgan, Gary Owen, David Greig, Philip Ridley, Douglas Maxwell, Enda Walsh, Gregory Burke. Many of these writers have received subsequent commissions from national and regional theatres, film and television companies here and abroad.

At the end of 2004 Paines Plough appointed its eighth Artistic Director, Roxana Silbert. She joins the company in January 2005 ready to lead us into our next exciting phase.

If you would like to be on Paines Plough's free mailing list, please send your details to:

Helen Poole
Paines Plough, 4th Floor, 43 Aldwych, LONDON WC2B 4DN
T + 44 (0) 20 7240 4533
F + 44 (0) 20 7240 4534
office@painesplough.com
www.painesplough.com

Paines Plough is supported by:

Paines Plough are:

Artistic Director	Roxana Silbert
General Manager	Kerry Whelan
Associate Director	John Tiffany
Literary Manager	Lucy Morrison
Projects Manager	Susannah Jeffries
Administrator	Helen Poole
Assistant Director (Arts Council England)	Hamish Pirie
Associate Playwright (Arts Council England)	Dennis Kelly
Pearson Writer in Residence	Chloe Moss

Board of Directors:

Roanna Benn, Tamara Cizeika, Giles Croft, David Edwards (Chair), Chris Elwell (Vice Chair), Fraser Grant, Clare O'Brien, Jenny Sealey.

Paines Plough would like to thank the following, without whom This Other England would not have been possible:

Alan Brodie	Tamara Cizeika
Robert Kent & Blinkhorns	Nick Eliott
Casarotto Ramsay	Joachim Fleury
Carolyn Bonnyman	Alison Richie
Tricia Mahoney	A D Penalver
David James	Kacey Ainsworth
The Agency	David Aukin and Nancy Meckler
Robbie Jarvis	Sheila Reid
Ashley Pharoah	Antoine Dupuy D'Angeal
Kim Oliver	David Bradshaw
Ann Bowen	Miranda Sawyer
Alan Ayckbourn	Trudie Styler
Adam Kenwright Associates	Old Vic New Voices

THE SMALL THINGS

Enda Walsh

Characters

MAN

WOMAN

Heavy red velvet curtains open slowly to the sound of a loud dramatic drumroll on timpani drums.

At the front of the large stage are two armchairs beside each other, sort of faced towards each other.

In one of them sits an elderly MAN, *his age indecipherable, his face worn and tired. He wears a cardigan and a shirt and bow tie. His trousers a little worn. Surprisingly, he wears a very polished pair of small black children's shoes with red laces. His expression like a bemused clown. He holds a battered wind-up clock and stares at it.*

In the other armchair is an old tape recorder.

To the left and behind the MAN, *a* WOMAN *sits at a small oak table with a lace tablecloth, polishing twelve small ceramic animals lined up in a row. Her age again difficult for us to gauge, her face a little tired and loose. She wears a house coat over a plain skirt and blouse and a pair of slippers. Similarly to the* MAN, *in front of her is a wind-up clock, though hers is immaculate.*

On the back wall of the stage is an enormous window/screen. A yellow-grey light emanates from it and light moves slowly in and out of shadow like cloud passing.

The two sit for a while doing very little as the sound of the drums continues loud.

She looks over towards the window.

The drumroll suddenly stops with a flourish.

WOMAN (*to the window*). Window. Knickknacks. Song.

His clock sounds. He slaps it off and begins.

MAN. It's been raining for the past two weeks which
would account for dampness. Not that I could
remember. How could I remember. Impossible to
remember! But dampness is there, its cause forgotten
but dampness is everywhere. My shoes on the parquet
floor and mother's shoes in front. We're marching me
and her. Parquet floor zigzagging down corridors. I
understand my damp hands as fear and I'm sort of
crying. I had cried in car but forgotten I was upset.
But in crying now I remember the tears of before and
remember that this day's primary feelings are fear, you
see. Fear. Each salty tear a reminder, each clammy
hand putting me in my place. Mother's heels on hard
floor, anxious. Marking out seconds. They're
alternating tween her tight breath and beat of heels.
The clip clop, the tight breath. The clip clop. My
breath.

He pants three times and stops.

I'm three years old and all talk is me and future and
books and learning and I'd be lying if I said I wasn't
excited because in truth I'm dead excited. I'm leaving
behind a life that's somewhat lumpen – HEY!

*He stops and suddenly writes in a small notebook with
a pencil.*

Fine word 'lumpen'. A single rhyme with pumpkin,
love. (*Closes the notebook.*) For what are babies but
lumps. Happy lumps granted but lumpen and sat still
all day much like I am sat right now. Difference tween
babies and me, is lumpen babies must give in to life
while my giving in will be to death. One a cheery
departure and one not so cheery . . . though in honesty
which one is which. Slight joke. No need for slight

jokes when no one's laughing, the bastards! The clip
clop stops. She kneels in front of me. She hugs me.
She kisses me on cheek. Starts telling me to enjoy my
day but all this time I'm looking right down her
blouse. I never loved my mother in that way. Never
had feelings of . . . feelings of lust . . . too strong, easy
now . . . lust?!! . . . feelings of . . . ? . . . I know what
I mean! Frankly she was never very loving to me. That
hug in the classroom an unusual show of affection
more to do with doing right thing than telling me of
her love, self-pity, very attractive in an old man.

He laughs. She laughs.

Oh very good! Very nice!

They both stop laughing.

I drop my school bag and reach in and hold my
mother's breasts.

WOMAN. Oh!

MAN. It's an action that lasts all of a split second and at
first I'm amazed that the motion is so fluid for a three
year old and that I make contact so precisely and also
that in my hands both titties weigh exact same measure.
This is my moment! Beginning of my professional
life. Yes! Before she slaps my hands away and belts
me across head, before my new classmates burst into
laughter and I start my journey into a childhood of
ridicule and psychological torture, not true, though
interesting! Before any of this shite and it's just me
with Mother's tits held in perfect symmetry in my
hands . . . at that moment I promise myself a life in
engineering. I am ready . . . for order.

He looks at the clock. She's looking at her clock.

WOMAN. I'm up out of bed and flinging myself through
house like a mad thing, like a rag doll. And downstairs

dragging sweaty fingers down walls. Into kitchen and a breakfast scene. Dozy-chat mixing with pop music off radio – ding-a-ling. Cornflakes crunching above the quiet din of breakfast time and all is a deadly normal but for Dad's face. Dad's face! Crikey! He's been complaining about a headache for the past month! Last week Mother caught him staring at the clouds, staring at the birds and shaking his head and mumbling to himself, 'What chaos in the world. What terrible chaos.' I saw him walking around town in dead straight lines while all around the world is going about the day-to-day business of accident and chance. Accident and chance, them two words churning Dad's stomach. This morning and his eyes are stuck out of his face like they want to be rid of his head. Still sat in his jim-jams he pours the cornflakes out onto table, sits there and starts to count them out one by one. Sets out cornflakes into a neat square and my brother starts to giggle. An orange square and the disorder of the cornflakes are set to a pattern, you see. Well skip forward to dinner time, still sat in his jim-jams and he has us whispering our words. No dinner sounds and us all hushed and careful. He wipes the sauce off his spaghetti and lays spaghetti out into a simple grid-shape and for the first time we hear these new words, 'Where would any of us be without order, kids?'

MAN. Christ.

WOMAN. Suddenly it's us who's starting each day wondering where we'd be without order. What terrible shape the world would be if the great Lord hadn't such an appreciation for ordered things? 'Sending night after day and autumn to cool summer and all of those happy miracles.' Six years old and I thought that, then. Because of my father's persistence, order starts ruling the house. For one year timetables meet us each morning. Two watches for two naughty children laid out on table. Each task allotted time. An exact time for each task. Strap watches on and we slot into our routine. Can't remember exact times now. No can't. Not important. Hardly adds to the story! But the shape of the day. The rhythm of how it runs and how I run. A bloody odd sight, I tell ya! Two children, timetables alert being pushed about house by seconds, by minutes. And Father standing a foot behind always guiding and watching. 'Watching and guiding! Watching and guiding!' My four-year-old brother spends too long washing the dishes and I'm looking at my father standing over him screaming at the back of his head. Not words just this long scream, right here.

She indicates where on the head and screams.

MAN. Easy.

WOMAN. The day after that there was no timetables out. Mother sat in bed with Father, 'Things will be all right, Martin.' At night I can hear him sobbing and saying how sorry he is that he screamed at my brother but really we'd be lost without our timetables. Lost without 'the order of the routine, Maureen.' And it's true, at first I am lost! No timetable and I stand in house searching for routine. It's me who's stood behind my brother now and screaming at the back of his head. Monkey see monkey do. In this little scene the familiar feeling safe strangely. (*Screams. Stops.*) Safe but wrong, surely, what with my brother's tears. I start panicking a little and face my stopwatch and counting the seconds as they leave me. Useless and stood still and unable to figure out the day. But at least there's order in the seconds, hey?! One two three four five six and so on . . . At least some pattern to keep safe!

MAN. Yap yap yap!

WOMAN. I'm sitting on the couch dead still and silent
    and watching the seconds and holding my breath for
    fear that my breath might blow the seconds to God
    knows where! It's the worry of the uncertain, as Dad
    might say. You start an action that effects another and
    then another and pretty soon life turns into chaos.
    'Look at them clouds! Formless and blowing about!
    It's bloody anarchy up there!' So it's best to keep
    inside and sat on couch and do nothing at all. Well
    fuck that! I have to stop those thoughts because that's
    where madness lies and Mother says that one mad
    person in house is bad enough and it's best to go
    outside and investigate the village like any other normal
    girl should. Which I do. (*About a small ceramic cat.*)
    Now this is the fella I talk to!

MAN. Were you listening to my first story?

WOMAN. All of them I talk to at some stage, of course.

MAN. Wasn't it short on detail today?

WOMAN. Not conversations obviously for really it's all
    one way, don't be daft.

MAN. Hey?

WOMAN. It's always one-way conversations with me
    and my knickknacks, isn't it, boys! But you know
    I stopped talking to them because of . . . (*Stops.*)
    Actually I can't remember why I stopped talking to
    them. (*Rattled.*) Boredom, of course, but that's no
    reason. Boredom's not a good enough reason. Sure
    boredom's got the run of me, hasn't it! Beyond
    boredom I am and shaped from a much more boring
    place than just your everyday run of the mill, 'Fuck
    me, I'm bored!' So it's not likely that it could be
    boredom. Though you never know. Doesn't seem
    likely or logical, mind you.

MAN (*staring at the clock and shaking it*). Tickatocka-tickatocktickatockatickatocktickatockatickatock!

WOMAN. Seems strange that I would stop talking to the knickknacks, doesn't it? Christ, I'll have to rectify that one and slot it back into the day. Once it's not taking away from the stories! Once the clock and the stories allow for some idle chit chat with the knickknacks then where's the harm, do you get me?!

MAN. Not really.

WOMAN. But, anyway, *this* fella I talked to on account of his inquisitive face. Ya cheeky! Look at that! He always has a cleverer look than me. Especially. At. This. Very. Moment.

Silence as they do very little. Suddenly the sound of the timpani drum as it builds to a flourish. It stops.

His clock sounds again and he slams it off and resumes.

MAN. I leave my house and slam the front door with an imprint of Mother's hand on face.

WOMAN (*looking at clock*). What?

MAN. Little stiffness still in pants. My short pants. The pants that dug into my prick on account of new zip. The second hand zip, yes Mother, removed from somewhere or other and welded onto these shorts and making my summer-life a misery, by the way. Yes misery, Mother! A chafing misery! This morning worst than normal though because of the stiffness. My six-year-old stiffness pressed against zip.

WOMAN (*staring at her clock. Sighs*). Fine.

MAN. I was sat on bed with Mother's bra laid out in front of me. Her room and it was the mothball smells

that had me in a daze for I couldn't hear her feet –
clip clop – on the stairs for everything was that lovely
bra. Well I had just placed my face into one of the
cups of the lovely bra . . . when bloody door flies open
and Mother's hand 'Schmack! Schmack! Schmack!',
me running for the door, for the front door then
and outside outside-outside-outside-outside-outside-
outside . . .

WOMAN. And outside to village for me and, 'Oh isn't it
great to be finally in the outside!' – skip skip – with
conversations . . . conversations about absolutely
nothing. I stand there for minutes with all talk leading
to nowhere, imagine that! All order is bent out of
shape in the outside. The world made up of this small
talk and listening to the words trail off to . . . where
ever words go to. To nothing maybe. To nowhere
maybe. To . . . to . . . (*Reprimanding herself.*) I really
mustn't think those thoughts and get back! Chin up,
woman. You allow Mr Glum inside you'll be booking
your ticket to that road down below, the bastard.
'Where's this you're off to?'

MAN. Out. Just out.

WOMAN. Your mother's well, isn't she?

MAN. She is, yeah. She's fine.

WOMAN. You look nice. A little dressed up, mind you.
Chit chat.

MAN. They're my Sunday clothes.

WOMAN. Are you off to Church Fete then?

MAN. I am as a matter of fact. Chit chat chit chat.

WOMAN. Off to Church Fete?

MAN. Chit chat chit chat. (*He laughs.*)

MAN *and* WOMAN. Chit chat chit chat. Chit chat chit chat. Chit chat chit chat. Chit chat chit chat. Chit chat chit chat.

WOMAN (*laughing*). She can see where I'm at and where I'm off to! A plate full of meringues, look!! With cellophane all wrapped them, woman!?

MAN (*quiet*). Tick tock tick tock.

WOMAN. It's not like I'm off directly to the new swimming pool, is it?! Got me inflatable armbands for that job! Won't get far in the pool wearing these meringues, will I?! Bottom of the swimming pool with the meringues! How could you forget about them meringues?

MAN. Meringues can never be forgotten.

WOMAN. Sure that silly cow was just making the small talk, bless her. The sound of this village played out in everyone's words, hey. Maybe only fifty of us livin' here and our voices all stuck in same music. Close my eyes, it's like listening to myself as I walk through village. Skipping through broken chit chat towards fete in field at back of church.

MAN. What time do you think it is?

WOMAN. Ohh the lovely sound of those words and the shape of the small talk! And days have their very own sound, don't they?! The way people talk on the Sunday decidedly different from the Friday talk. One all restless and shapeless, the other a little languid somehow. Fantastic word 'languid'. I'll use it again before the day runs out.

The clock sounds its alarm again and again he slams it off.

MAN. I am stood at the big table . . .

WOMAN. Languid. Genius.

MAN. . . . my eyes full of cakes and buns. I'm looking at different shapes of cakes with a young engineer's critical eye. My mouth's already bubbling up with spit, with expectation for the cream, for the sponge. I didn't have breakfast this morning so even the shortbread's looking half decent, though structurally a little unsound, not true, no matter, carry on! But then I see the meringues! Those lovely magnificent gable-shaped cakes!

Slight pause.

It's not lost on me that yet again it's Mother's breasts I'm thinking about as I look down on those meringues . . . so I buy two . . . shove one in my mouth.

WOMAN. The meringue's halfway in and that's when you look at me.

A pause.

MAN (*to himself. Whispers*). Meringues.

A pause.

WOMAN. My mother made them.

MAN. Did she? Crikey. They're lovely.

WOMAN. I helped her to.

MAN. Did ya? You did a good job. They're delicious. How come I haven't seen you about village chit chat?

WOMAN. My dad likes to keep us locked inside house. That's all finished though. From here on in, I'm outside house.

MAN. What about a dip in that new swimming pool?

WOMAN. And you're dragging me by the hand and pulling the arm off me! The words too fast in your

mouth spitting out all the things you're about to do in
life. Into swimming pool and the voices of other
children smacking off the tiles and you and me
strippin' off into our underpants. You jabbering on
about this and that! And it's like my last year locked in
the house and stuck in Dad's routines is soon forgotten.
My childhood returned with your talk of life and loves
and hates. Christ but you're a talker!

MAN. I can't stop talking, me! I'm like my Aunty Ada!
A woman who wore her teeth out with all her chat.
Who had a jaw the size of a small car with all that
bloody talk. Never held hands with a girl before so in
its excitement my brain is packing bullshit into my
gob. I'm all 'me this and me that'! I'm coming across
as a right little pain in the arse. Zip into shop and buy
some penny chews just to bung me up but I can't stop
the talk! You bobbing along beside, your little blue
eyes smiling at me all innocent yet cheeky. We're into
pool and I'm strippin' off my pants like a mad thing.
Six years old I'm already thinking of us sharing a bed
and making babies, getting married and getting the
decorators in. What's got into me!? I'm thinking all
this but talking structural engineering all of a sudden. I
have to stop talking and get splashing. Get splashing!

WOMAN. Into pool then with these nicked inflatable
armbands and aren't we skinny. The cold water goose-
bumping our little arms, look!

MAN. I look like I'm made from chicken! Isn't skin a
wonder all the same?!

WOMAN. We're facing each other doing the doggy
paddle and you cross your eyes and make a face.
Momentarily I think you've gone spastic on me but
that soon passes and you're smiling once more like a
normal child.

MAN. I never was one for comedy but always felt the need to give it a go.

WOMAN. You can't stop talking, can ya! You're like a factory for words and I can't stop smiling at ya!

MAN. I'm Aunty Bloody Ada, that's who!

He laughs a little.

WOMAN. The pool clears and we're left alone, hey.

A pause. Slower.

We're like the last two people alive, me and you. We imagine we are. We think about us being the last two and what fun we might have in that world. We don't say much and just bob about.

MAN. Truth is, my six-year-old jaw's all worn out from the chat and the penny chews. Feels good to stay quiet for a bit.

A long pause.

Dried off now and we walk back outside to the sun and the lure of the Church Fete and those meringues on the cake table.

WOMAN. Walk side by side and the conversation settling into this easy rhythm. You're less of the jabbering spastic and I'm finding words I never thought I had. Our words equal fold around each other and I suppose we're at ease now. It's all good. It's all . . . ? . . . nice.

Slight pause.

That day we're bonded me and you. The day of the no timetable. The day of the no stopwatch. The day of the no routine.

Slight pause.

We're standing back at the cake table.

Slight pause.

Dad's standing next to me suddenly. Takes me by the hand.

A pause.

His knuckles are bruised and bloody.

She turns away from the clock.

MAN. I've been thinking about other things so much that maybe it's started this . . . ? . . . 'thing'. Seems possible that all these new thoughts may be the cause of what's happening inside. Not sure who it is talking inside of me. Give him a name and you prove he's alive . . . so not quite ready to give who it is inside a name just yet?

Looks at his hands and whispers.

I'm no longer six years old . . . nor twelve even . . . that much is true. Are you listening to me?

A pause.

WOMAN. Yes.

MAN. How can I be sure?

A pause.

WOMAN. I'm here, aren't I?

MAN. Yeah but how can I be certain you're listening?

WOMAN. Good question.

He looks down at his clock. He resumes.

MAN. You leave with your dad.

Slight pause.

I see the other children run into woods and it's like my legs take me after them. All squealing inside with trees

and us all busy, all fast. No order inside there. Time
bent out of shape. Our world given over to blurry
browns and gold and laughter. (*Whispers.*) Nice words
them.

Pause.

He's lying face down, his clothes off him. We get a big
stick and roll his body over. Dead leaves stuck on his
front like some fancy vest. His blood black, his fingers
thick with muck, his face smashed up but we all know
him well. His father owns chip shop in the village and
he works there on Saturdays. His mouth open . . . you
can see his teeth smashed up from the thumping he
got.

Slight pause.

The chip-shop man has killed his only son. Cut out his
tongue and smashed him up.

Slight pause.

He gave me a free battered sausage once.

WOMAN (*staring at clock*). What time do you think it
is?

MAN. I think I'll sit a while and listen to him talking
inside a me.

WOMAN (*quietly. Excited*). That time.

MAN. I'll decide whether it's time to give him a name
and be done with it all. (*Whispers.*) I'll decide whether
it's time to give him a name and be done with this life.

Slight pause.

Do I really mean what I say . . . ? . . . or have these
words got the run of me completely?

He's frightened now. Snaps.

Fuck it.

The MAN *closes his eyes but immediately opens them and stares down at his clock.*

Tentatively she turns the face of the clock away from her. She breathes a sigh of relief.

WOMAN. Just before going to the window I torture myself with a little silence! Which isn't very nice and a bit difficult but nature calls for a pause. Such is sleep. When sleep finally arrives – lazy bastard. You can't move forward lest you stop now and again, can ya? Take stock. Otherwise it's just moving willy-nilly. Take these little fellas. A constant polish just wears them out. Better to let dust settle. Ya can't be handling the knickknacks willy-nilly, can you? Wear out the little beggers. Give them a breath. A little stand still. Just look at that face on the inquisitive one. Right? Yeah? Well aware he is of my next move so why the questioning face? I've got every right to wipe that look right off ya, ya little! Anyway, as much as I try for silence I seem to fall short on account of this talking.

Pause. She looks over to the window and smiles a little.

Right about this time I allow myself some action!

She stands up from her seat. A little uneasy, she waits until she has her balance.

Nothing in the world quite like a little action to get the blood racing.

She then walks very slowly towards the window. Whispers to herself.

Window window window! Suddenly 'possibility' shows its happy head.

Slight pause.

Now look how I walk, sweetheart. My speed . . . lack
of . . . position of my head bent towards floor . . . body
a little tight . . . in . . . in . . . in? . . . it may look like
constipation . . . it is in fact in anticipation. Hardly my
greatest performance but it's found me nearing the
window once again. The window. My look then! My
look . . . ? . . . my look a little hungry at first, probably.
It is the window after all and not the deadness of the
walls. Warrants some joy. It does offer . . . a perspective,
definitely, what window doesn't?! . . . and dare I say a
bigger hope. Try to ignore my dodgy legs as they root
me to this floor, raising the head to look towards and
out of the window like a fat man acknowledging a
meat supper . . .

Finally she looks out the window.

. . . and there it is! The house in the distance on top of
that mountain. Our two houses blinking over at each
other . . . over the . . . ? . . . (*Thinks.*) . . . Oh the world
that was there, that's enough. That silent road below.
The sea.

Slight pause.

Small house much like this house. Wooden-panelled,
same as this – very nice. Mind you, I haven't seen the
outside of this place for an age and it may be covered
in another form for all I know. Ice-cream wafers!
(*Laughs a little.*) Hardly. But that house. I can
sometimes see a figure sitting by the . . .

Pause as she looks out.

I can imagine all sorts of life in that house. Lively chit
chat as the night gets closer. Music. I should have
never burnt that piano! Other things could have been
burnt. The bloody knickknacks, for example! What
music do they give me but the daily inquisition. The
daily reminder! The piano was an innocent. Day I

arrived in here . . . it was there, sat in the corner, all
wise and full of history and loved once most certainly.
I tried playing it for the first few months but it was
bloody murder. Fel' like music itself was dying. Like
these sausage fingers were drumming out the death
march! Well if it wasn't for the tape recorder, wasn't
for your song, sweetheart, I might have felt like all
music was six foot under! Getting ahead of myself!
No mention of the song before before . . . easy easy
easy! But that house. Come on!! Come on!!

Slight pause. Covering her ears and concentrating.

Such music there. Something lively now. Something
that would give my veins a good draining, the
floorboards a pounding . . . a celebration for . . . ?
Well not for anything in particular but for the sake of
a difference . . . a different life . . . something? . . . can
the word 'frivolous' still be used despite everything?
I don't see why not! Something frivolous is happening
in that house. Something frivolous is happening!

Laughs a little. Pause.

It was only the one figure I saw, mind . . . and now
gone . . . mustn't get too glum, come on! CHRIST!
We all know where glum gets me . . . a longer day for
starters. I mean, I do have some fun times in here.
Hardly a holiday camp, granted, but we do have the
odd giggle, don't we, sweetheart, hey? Remember that
day when you . . . and it was . . . and you did that . . .
and I was . . . and before we know it . . . it was all . . .

She laughs. The MAN *remains silent. She suddenly
stops laughing.*

(*Downbeat.*) Oh it's too easy to wear out these
glorious moments by the window! Enough then.

*She turns away from the window and walks back to
her seat.*

MAN (*looks down at his shoes*). Look how they remind
me. These! These funny children's shoes. All these
years . . . just following me.

The timpani drumroll begins to fade up.

Reminding me . . .

*The drumroll finishes with a flourish. His clock sounds
and again he slaps it off and resumes.*

'But I don't want sauce, I like them salty.' 'Sauce is
salty, ya daft bugger!' 'They make the chips soggy like
slugs.' 'What's wrong with slugs? Are you being a
naughty boy?' My little heartbeat then. And him and
me know what he's talking about. Find myself saying
'brown'. Fixes me with his look and covers my chips
in that brown tangy shite and turning the chips to
slugs. He's backing me into the wall now and him
holding my soggy chips and joking about his naughty
son who needed silence the other day, didn't he, who
needed the routine like the boss man said. 'But stood
up against his own dad!' So then kicked in, weren't
he! Kicked in! I watch the chip-shop man take t'street
outside with this new power. He walks the road and
it's like he sucks in all life about him. Holds my soggy
chips up to the sky and fucks them against a shop
window. It's his time, it's his time.

She looks at her clock.

WOMAN. I'm sat in living room listening to Father and
the chip-shop man. And Father's big idea they talk.
They talk about spreading the silence. How quiet and
peaceful the village will be without words. How
perfect the world without this chit chat. Over a cup of
tea they speak about the naughty boy and how they
sliced his tongue off. My timetable they gave him and
the routine that kept him. The routine making him. For
a week my timetable marking this boy's every breath

'til he stood up. 'So kicked in, weren't he. Kicked in.'
I look at Mother looking at Dad's bruised and bloody
knuckles. And her too bashed down to talk up. Her
words are stuck in her throat as she carves up the
coffee cake. It starts. It begins.

MAN. Mother pulls me aside – clip clop clip clop – and
tells me now's the time to grow up fast. She tells me
not to be scared. But I am scared. 'Don't be scared,
love.' 'I'm scared of the chip-shop man.' Strikes me
across face, throws her hands to her eyes and she's the
one who cries! Well fuck this, I'm outside-outside-
outside-outside-outside . . .

WOMAN. And just me and you alone in village walking
towards each other and a secret I have to tell.

MAN. Something's happening here.

WOMAN. It's my dad and the chip-shop man. Only the
bad ones will be silenced, so don't be scared?

MAN. 'But I am scared!' And walk through woods and
pass where they took up the boy's body. Instead of
him there, someone has put a bunch of flowers. I bend
down and pick up a red carnation and hand it to ya. A
romantic gesture for a six year old. Though in
hindsight a jot morbid.

WOMAN. Take my hand then and let's walk down to
river at the other end of woods.

MAN. Each step and another month and a year passes.
For six years I'm by your side.

WOMAN. Six years it passes with my dad and the chip-
shop man slicing the tongues.

MAN. And we talk about those ten people who've been
silenced already. We watch them walk about the
village with clipboards and stopwatches. They walk in

little trenches the chip-shop man dug. Like train tracks
the trenches are and stuck in patterns the Silent shuffle
along all funny-looking. We laugh about the routines
they're given. An alarm sounds and we see a man
stood outside a house and made to count the bricks.
Another man stood behind this man made to count the
seconds it takes the man to count the bricks. An alarm
sounds and we see a woman stand in a field counting
bees, counting birds, counting flies, a man made to
measure all that can be measured in the village.
Another man marking the time it takes this man to
measure these things 'til that's his order for everyday
after. An alarm sounds and I see a woman made to
count her breaths in a single day making that number
of breaths her marker for all of her days. An alarm
sounds . . .

WOMAN. Shhhh.

*He covers his mouth with his hands, stopping the
words. A pause. He lowers his hands.*

We sit in our spot. Two little twelve year olds by
river's edge. Turn away from what the village's been
turned into and we lose ourselves in our secret chat.
Our talk all shapeless and trailing off to where ever
words go to. Just talk nonsense talk, really. The sort of
talk that has my dad feeling sick. Talk ourselves stupid
'til we give into silence. In these moments by the river
we happily give into silence.

MAN. A kiss.

WOMAN. And kiss then. And lie down into autumn
leaves you set up like a mattress. The little light about
us too, a jigsaw of browns and golds, isn't it? All talk
is gone with your easy breath against my stomach.
The river sounds led by your breath. I sleep. Lost in a
dream of some happy house on a mountain . . . they
were my dreams back then. I'm sleeping.

MAN (*grimaces*). That will be my insides scheming. Whatever they're saying it takes me by the second. I try to listen but the talking is buried deep. Might I be able to hear it soon? For right now I wonder the purpose of this telling once again.

Pause.

Still.

He stares down at his clock and silently mouths as the seconds pass until he must speak again. Quietly then.

You sleep with the river sounds led by your breath. The little currents whirring all easy, the popping sounds ebbing up and down. I turn and look towards river.

Slight pause.

I'm looking at the chip-shop man standing right by your mother and he's pulling at her hair. She's kneeling in the water and her eyes staring right over at me. Those ten others who are already silenced are stood by the bank looking on all dumb with clipboards and stopwatches. He takes a kitchen knife to her tongue. Blood all down her pinny and he shoves her under the water. Your dad drags her out and holds her up to the others like some wet puppy.

Slight pause.

'Reborn,' he says. All polite applause. Little applause. Your mother's looking over at me. The Silent are looking at us.

WOMAN. Right about this time I remind myself to stay happy! Well not happy! Don't be ridiculous! Happy! (*Laughs.*) What's the word? (*She can't think of it.*) Now don't fail me. Christ, imagine that nightmare!

Each second passing and another word abandons ship
and then where would I be? Stuck in goo-gaa words.
The brain turned to slush and me the picture of old
age. Little dribble out side of mouth and mumbling
out the inane! Little dusty smells crawling out my
backside unannounced! Shuffling across lino with all
the speed of slugs! Hah! Actually closer to that image
than I'd like to be. But right about this time I remind
myself to stay 'confident'. Confident for what reason?
Now there's a question. The question. 'Cause without
confidence bloody fear would gobble me up and then
where would I be? Where would I be would not be
here. Here looking out window, across at that house
and hoping for . . . it doesn't matter what for, 'cause
really hope is enough to go on. To go on? To survive
by. Hope is certainly more than enough to survive by.
I've made it that way and to be honest I am of an age
to know nothing else – hint of pity in that voice! There
is only the chance of fear and the hope for something
marginally better than this existence. A moment of
honesty. (*Disciplining herself.*) 'Honesty'!! STOP
TALKING! STOP IT!

Pause.

It's time to turn that frown to upside down. Not the
song just yet but the knickknacks! Many moons ago
I happened upon another purpose for these fellas. A
purpose a lot more creative than being the recipients
of a good dusting every fifteen minutes. I made a show
for them. The story was . . . ? . . . such and such. I had
an ending but I threw it out. It didn't seem worthy of
the start. But I did like it though and it grew on me, so
I got rid of the start and was left with ending which
seemed unsatisfactory now that it didn't have a
beginning.

MAN (*groans*). Oh my God.

WOMAN. Without a start or an ending there was absolutely no reason to continue. But of course I did!

MAN. Of course.

WOMAN. For there will always be a reason. Though for the life of me I have no idea what it was chit chat chit chat! Anyway, everyday . . . I take a minute out to wait for the knickknacks to begin from 'the middle'. Free my mind of these stories and thoughts of madness and just . . . wait.

A long pause as she sits and stares at them.

Nothing just yet. A little stage-struck even now, bless 'em.

A long pause as she waits.

And still nothing just yet.

Another long pause as she stares waiting for the knickknacks.

Still nothing.

Another long pause. Finally her optimism breaks.

(*Quiet.*) Nothing.

MAN. When did this body stop? When I say this body, I mean the legs, of course. The rest is still intact and in order. Reasonably. But these chicken legs gave up the chase a little time ago. Body's way of telling me to stay put and think things through. Which I have been doing, thank you very much! Which has become my everything. This thinking things through. But why not just other thoughts? The here and the now. Luxury. Her about me and fussing about me and making my tea . . . of course there's never any tea . . . but us lost in our chit chat, you know. Why not only these small things?

Slight pause.

I'll whisper so the shoes can't listen.

Slight pause. He whispers slowly.

Am I ready . . . to give in? Am I ready . . . to be silenced?

His clocks sounds and he wrestles with it and then sits on it to block out the noise.

Looking at her clock she resumes.

WOMAN. We're sat on the couch eating chips. Mother standing in the corner where the telly was. She's faced towards wall like a bad girl. I'm watching her pudgy hands shaking by her side, little snivelling noises from her silent gob. She's heard something from Dad and the chip-shop man. She knows why we're in our swimming togs and waiting this past hour. Me and my brother sat there eating the soggy chips and thinking about the swimming pool. Oh it has to be the swimming pool. No other reason for this baggy swimsuit. Fuck it, I look like I'm sheddin' skin. The crotch that baggy, I'm a little undecent to be honest. Little breasts like garden peas, I'm a right state!

His clock has stopped and, delighted, he takes it back into his hands and shakes it in triumph.

MAN. YES!

WOMAN. We're outside with Dad marching behind us. I look at my little brother still juggling with his chips. The brown sauce spitting onto his belly and he's dead excited! 'You love the swimming pool, don't ya? Into your inflatable tortoise and you'll be in the pool 'til Christmas.' My little feet pinching on the road. We're walking over all those trenches that are dug for those Silent Ones. Father, the big engine, marching us down

street, 'Where would any of us be without order?
What greatness this silence. What wonder the routine.'
Blah blah blah BLAH BLAH BLAH BLAH BLAH
BLAH BLAH BLAH! WE WALK!

*His clock sounds and again he slaps it off and
resumes.*

MAN. I'm woken by the chip-shop man. His fat face
telling me to, 'Get t' pool, naughty boy! Get to pool!'
He sits on my bed and watches me change into my
togs, the dirty fuck! And we're stood outside the
swimming pool. The children from the village, all
twenty of us standing in our togs. And what a state we
are! Like a box of fish fingers with skin all bluey
white. Little skinny arms wrapped around against cold.
I'm stood next to some fourteen-year-old bloke
bursting out of his trunks. Crikey! Spiky pubic hair,
the very look of fills my belly with jealousy. Look at
my own wretched sack. Bald but for a single hair and
sat in my briefs like a tiny canary egg. Bloody shame!
THE SHAME! It's these togs, isn't it?! Togs that I've
been wearing since the age of eight, yes Mother!
Making my every trip to the swimming pool a torture,
Mother! I'm standing there clamped into these 'baby-
blue panties' and shame shaping out a slug for a prick!
Tramp-tramp-tramp-tramp-tramp-tramp! I see you
being marched up the main street. Your dad marching
behind. Your little brother, he's that covered in brown
sauce he looks like he's shat himself. And he's
laughing but we know what's what.

WOMAN. The children huddled together and you make
some apology for your tight trunks and I just smile at
you and hold your hand.

MAN. A surprise then. My one and only gift to you.

WOMAN. What's this?

MAN. I made it for you last night, didn't I.

WOMAN. We can listen to it later in yours.

MAN. Tape recorder shoved against the speaker in the front room. It's proper good!

WOMAN. What do you mean there mightn't be a later?

MAN. Are you listening to me?

WOMAN. I take the tape and hide it in my baggy costume. Keep it safe this lovely tape and hold your hand while we watch the men and women of the village gather about with their faces full of the fear and listening to my dad droning on about spreading the silence even further. Droning on – droning on – droning on!

MAN. Tick tock tick tock!

WOMAN. Stood in our togs and the chip-shop man hoses us down all of a sudden. Hands to our faces and we're dropping to our knees for covered in petrol.

MAN. And that fourteen-year-old boy's dragged out. And what a little child, all of a sudden he looks like a little girly standing there. Soaked in petrol and stood in front of his mum and dad with his little girly cries! The boss man's words and telling his parents to take their tongues.

WOMAN. I watch my father holding the lighter I bought him for Christmas. I'm watching the boy's mam and dad take each other's tongues with knives and the boy saved.

MAN. It's all busy now with men and women trying to save their children. My mother stood beside the chip-shop man. Knives passed quickly and tongues cut out. Blood and all is bits with words giving over to tears and silence. I'm being dragged inside and I can see you hiding by your mother's side. You're gone from me. You're gone. A breath, a pause . . .

His clock sounds and he watches it for some time, exhausted. He slowly presses it off. He takes a breath. Slower then.

Inside the swimming pool it's screaming just like the outside. Tongues are being taken just like the grown-ups were. Little children covered in blood tossed into swimming pool. I'm looking at your little brother in his inflatable tortoise. He's bobbing up and down covered in blood and looking dead. Boss man tells me I'll be saved. His work has been done here. It's time to spread the good news from village to village.

He looks at his clock.

Look how these seconds are bullying me. Switching me on and off for fun.

He turns it over on his lap to hide the face.

Finished. I'm finished.

WOMAN. What reason the telling, hey? What purpose all this detail?

She stares at the clock and mouths the seconds until it is her time to continue.

I'm hid under my mother's coat. We're sat on the ground at the edge of the woods with all the other women. All of them made silent and one at a time taken to the woods. I'm seen by a man made silent some six years ago. I seen him around village with his clipboard and stopwatch bringing 'a proper order' to all things. He drags me away from Mother and into woods. I want to bite through my tongue and be done with it all. Shot bodies of old women thrown about the dead wood. Still in my baggy swimsuit and my feet pinching on something or other. He opens my mouth . . . holds out my tongue with his knife. Close my eyes. I feel him inside my mouth and feel him drag at my hair. Face pressed to ground and punching and fucking in equal measures, you know that sad scene.

Slight pause. Starts to laugh a little.

Turn my head and a deep daydream!

Slight pause.

I'm falling slowly through clouds. It's a good feeling and each cloud softer than next, passing me from one to other, you know. Like a breath on me almost. The clouds soft on my skin, I fall. And then through clouds and into blue and towards the world. And winds light they pass me from one to other like a feather I am. And I fall slow. And I look at the world as it comes to me and me to it. And I see the different greens of our valley, lovely shape of the countryside. Even from here I can see our little village and see the church and woods. I fall. Then into woods and slowly through leaves of beech trees and passed then quietly from branch to branch and arms take me and then I see that it's you. And we fall onto that mattress you made from leaves and I fold into lovely you and we speak. I speak to you, sweetheart.

Slight pause.

Like I'm speaking to you now.

Slight pause.

I can see his gun by my side.

She looks at the clock and smiles a little.

That song then.

She presses the tape recorder and we hear the voice of the MAN *when he was a twelve-year-old* BOY.

BOY. Here's a song. Let's try and learn these words, hey? I'll hold it near speaker.

The song plays. It's The Mills Brothers singing the comedy classic 'Nagasaki'. He can be heard trying to sing along with it. The words come very fast which gets him laughing.

She listens and occasionally tries to mouth some lyrics.

The lyrics sung:

Hot gingerbread and dynamite,
That's all there is at night,
Back in Nagasaki where the fellows chew tobaccky
And the women wicky-wacky-woo!

They got the ways that they entertain,
Would hurry a hurricane.
Back in Nagasaki where the fellows chew tobaccky
And the women wicky-wacky-woo!

In Fujiama, ya get a mama,
Then your troubles increase, boy!
In South Dakota you want a soda,
Hershy-Kershy ten cents piece.

They hug you and kiss you each night,
By jingo, boys, worth that price!
Back in Nagasaki where the fellows chew tobaccky
And the women wicky-wacky-woo!

At exactly 1 minute 41 seconds it comes to an abrupt end. She stops the tape and begins to rewind it.

MAN. Suddenly can't stop thinking of a cup of tea. Not tempting me or nothing but a happy brew. Soak my brittle scheming insides and send me back to the land of the living.

A pause. Grave suddenly.

I remember my last cup.

The tape stops and she kisses the recorder. She stands up.

Will you listen to me?

She goes to the window.

It was maybe a couple of weeks ago now and I'm in the kitchen and once again I'm chatting to you, hey. The kettle boiled and I wrap my hands around cup and remember the softness of your hand when I passed you that tape that last day . . . you held my hand, remember? I'm telling you this and walking towards the window to look out on the outside and up at that house on the mountain. No warning, really. So I'm a little surprised when I look out window and it's like the empty outside has jumped down my throat. Don't even hear the tea hit the floor – cup smash. Try talking to you but maybe you're not listening to me any more. Look across at that house for a little hope. But I'm too shook. 'Cause I'm standing there and looking down at what were villages, staring at what was life and that road I help build. And here I am with my future . . . me forever shuffling about with these children's shoes on, the room forever my country, little tracks scratched into this floor showing off my daily routine, my yearly routine, my life's routine. Well I'm away from the window fast and turn this chair and face against this wall as I am now. Got this empty body whispering about that terrible bad thing that I did, and it's my time!

Slight pause.

Can I allow our words to drown and die like that . . . like me, with me? Either way the words and I are fucked and the fight is lost and that road and sea waits for me. It's not a question of can I stop talking to you, love . . . I must give in.

She stands again looking out the window. The light darkening outside.

WOMAN. Best turn that frown to upside down.

Slight pause.

You allow Mister Misery through our door and I'll be dusting 'til Christmas . . . whenever that may be.

MAN. Can I leave you alone and just give in?

A long pause as they do very little.

Again these children's shoes pinching me. They know of their arrival soon. Mocking me daily, the bastards!

WOMAN. For years I've passed the very same day just for moments like these. Today feeling different, though. I need to know you're listening to me still.

She turns from the window. She's been crying.

Are you?

A slight pause.

MAN. Yes.

WOMAN. Let me finish to this point! Deep breath, I'll reach the end and find some strength for another day.

She walks back to sit down in her armchair next to him. They both hold their alarm clocks.

They turn to each other and for the very first time their eyes meet.

MAN. Continue for the final time then. Begin.

The timpani drum begins to sound. The drumroll builds in volume and suddenly cuts.

Looking at her clock she resumes.

WOMAN. The ground all loose underneath and deeper
    into woods I run. Drop his gun and by the river I run.
    To where? To what plan? Can still taste that fucker
    in my mouth so spit out. Still soreness all about,
    so quicken my speed. What thoughts? No thoughts.
    Run 'til I can't run no more. And night to day and
    back to night. And a shell of me I am. No tears yet.
    No fear even. No feelings of fear. Just this running.
    No feelings of being alive. The daylight merely
    switching me on and off for fun. And night to day
    and back to night. And night to day and back to night.
    My sharp breath, my heart thumping, my legs chewing
    up soil. Through forest and moorland and steep hills
    now flat to my speed. Through meadows and farm
    and wind from the fells no match for me, I run. For
    days I run. My breath.

She pants for a few seconds and stops.

The rhythm of the run offering me thoughts that come
in pictures and each one is your sweet face and me
being pulled away from you. Each picture of you and
I lose you a little more. Each yard away is yard away
from you. And I stop with days of running behind. I'm
stood in heather and bilberry, my legs all jelly, my
face raw from wind and I'm trying to imagine you by
my side. I'm trying to place your kiss how it used to
be, try to hear your voice, try to remember our words
but the wind unkind it blows sweet remembered words
to where ever words float to. Kiss your tape then! This
tape! A little bit of you kept safe! You're gone from
me and for the first time I say those words, 'Are you
listening? Are you listening to me?'

His clock sounds and he slams it off.

MAN. Four boys taken out from the swimming pool with
    our voices saved. For what reason are we saved?
    Outside the pool and all is men made dumb. They

carry out the man you shot his balls and he wasn't too happy when they fell out the end of his trousers. The boss man stood up on a car and shouting his big talk. 'What great clarity this silence! Men giving over to simple routines and finding a function for once. Nature given an order.' He starts talking about a new order. A road that we must build. 'A road for the Silent. A road that will cut through the countryside and carry us lucky ones to Paradise.' And we march away with the village behind left all bloody and empty. March with other villages in our sights. And night to day and back to night. And night to day and back to night. Days turn to weeks and little villages torn up and other people made silent but for what reason do I still have my voice? The Silent grow. The road the road the road the road! And set to work. The road a constant. No pause for night even. And what freedom the road gives to my body. Shot to life I am. Is this my moment?! The great engineer! My life given a reason by this road. Now that you're gone from me a direction through this great road I build, my back stronger, arms shovelling the road faster than the other children. Legs marking out my new future with each step. And it's me in front of the others shouting just like the boss man does. My face no longer all frightened, fuck no! Now the little lap dog I am. The shifty little grin to the chip-shop man. Kneel in front, take his hand and kiss his pudgy hand. And is that a kindly pat on my head? The boss man dresses me up so that I'm stood apart from the dumb. The road flattening the green, and with each yard travelled it's more him I am than me. Again! It's more him I am than me!

WOMAN. The walk takes me its own course. Funny little legs led by the what-ifs. Driven slower but no less easier. No respite even. I'm looking for what? No answers. No questions to start. Just this aimless walking. I'm a child. Our village long gone, I rest in some wood. What was your face? Is it months? Is it really months past since? Heart more numbed than heavy. A breath for fear I'll blow up. A breath a pause a breath.

A pause.

The noise of a road being built in the distance behind. A little boy running scared from his village. Tells me about the men with knives who've come to bring silence and spread routine. The road they're building towards Paradise. Visions of my dad sitting at the breakfast table counting out those cornflakes making that orange square.

Pause.

I ask the boy to speak of other things and he does. I close my eyes and listen to those words returned. I tell him to make the small talk and just listen to the ebb and flow of those smaller words as he talks of the small things. And I talk too and our words entwine and with each word passed our old world is rebuilt somehow. The woods a bubble it keeps this hidden world safe and away from that road being built. And eyes still closed I take his face and I kiss him.

Slight pause.

I look at his shiny black shoes and red laces. Despite it all, a hope found in these funny little shoes.

Slight pause.

A boy calls his name.

His delivery slower too.

MAN. The road stopped by some woods. I enter with the boss man. 'A naughty boy ran off from that last village and he needs catching.' The boss man behind and I search the boy out. I call his name. I know now why my tongue has been saved. I call out for the boy and soon he comes running out towards me. He's all talk of another child that's nearby who needs saving too . . . a little girl he jabbers on about. I'm using my words to calm him. I'm using my words to lie to him. All the time I can see the boss man through the trees with his eyes on us. The kitchen knife he placed in my hand and to cut to the silence I push it far into the boy's mouth. I can't look at his face and stare down at his little black shoes and red laces.

A pause.

The boss man makes me put them on. 'Shoes fit for a Judas.' (*Breaking.*) And I am.

A pause. Outside is growing darker.

And run run run RUN RUN RUN RUN RUN RUN RUN!

WOMAN. And so begins my final run and where to this run? The screams of that boy in the distance and again the woods they take me and me through them.

MAN. And the woods through me I run away from that boy, away from that road. I run and through the woods.

WOMAN. And the woods no more and only this mountain to climb.

MAN. And higher I climb with that boy's face at every turn, with silence below and the road leading into the sea. The land emptying of the Silent with the boss man watching and guiding, guiding and watching as the Silent walk into the sea, their Paradise. I climb. And surely there's safety in the skies. And your face it guides me upwards. It takes me to where's safe.

WOMAN. And your face it guides me upwards and finds me this house and keeps me safe. It comforts me and opens my day and closes my night.

MAN. Inside this house and I lose myself in our past.

WOMAN. And I speak to you daily though you are not here and surely in the sea.

MAN. And speak to you daily though you are surely dead, love. Life passes and memory repeats.

WOMAN. Sat at table and mixing the meringues and looking at Mother at sink.

MAN. The parquet floor and my little heart all a flutter and Mother's breasts.

WOMAN. And the shape of town and speckled light and the gentle seasons passing.

MAN. And Mother's quilt and the smell of her bedroom and my face lost in that bra.

WOMAN. And the picture of the younger you standing at the cake table.

MAN. And bobbing about in my underpants talking like Aunty Ada. And the younger you. The lovely you and the river sounds and the stillness of us.

WOMAN. And your arms about me and sleep and your warm breath on my back.

MAN. And our mattress made from leaves.

WOMAN. And our mattress made from leaves.

MAN. Are you listening to me?

WOMAN. And are you listening to me?

MAN. Am I the last to talk?

WOMAN. 'Cause surely I'm the last.

MAN. Can I leave the words and find a proper sleep?

WOMAN. I am the last and yet the words much bigger than me. For words they float.

MAN. Us up in the skies spelt out in the small words and joined forever.

A long pause. They are still and silent.

WOMAN. I am alone here in this house though never quite alone. I pause. I feel fear. It subsides. The words trap and yet keep me. They float upwards and find their way as I find mine. Are you still speaking? Can I sleep?

Pause.

MAN. My insides are still now and wait. The outside silent, the world that was there not a stir, that house on that mountain and my house here, the cupboard without tea, the children's shoes, the road, the cold sea and Paradise . . . life and death paused then and wait for my choice.

Pause.

So what purpose my telling and what purpose me?

Pause.

To speak. (*Whispers to himself.*) To speak.

Pause. He smiles a little.

WOMAN. I can sleep then.

She closes her eyes and she vanishes from the space.

He is suddenly alone on the stage.

A long pause.

MAN. I'm alone here in my house . . . though never alone, hey love? I'll sleep and in the morning, as always, I'll continue . . . and I *will* speak . . . and we will live a life.

Pause.

Yes.

He closes his eyes as the timpani drum is faded up loud and the red velvet curtains slowly close.

Blackout.

The End.

A Nick Hern Book

The Small Things first published in Great Britain as a paperback original in 2005 by Nick Hern Books Limited, 14 Larden Road, London W3 7ST in association with Paines Plough

Cover Image: Stuart McCaffer

Typeset by Country Setting, Kingsdown, Kent CT14 8ES
Printed and bound in Great Britain by Bookmarque, Croydon, Surrey

A CIP catalogue record for this book is available from the British Library

ISBN 1 85459 843 0

Other Titles in this Series